I0483544

David Kravitz'
How to Monetize
Twitter, Facebook,
Snapchat, LinkedIn
and Other Social
Media Sites

by David Kravitz

Contents

Introduction

Social media platforms have successfully penetrated just about every industry in a very significant way, making a strong social media presence essential for any business that is serious about reaching consumers. Despite the overwhelming popularity of social media, many businesses are failing to properly take advantage of these platforms and have left a vacuum in which opportunities for monetization are quite abundant. Companies and individuals that have taken the time to develop a strong social media presence are now reaping the bulk of the reward when it comes to monetization while others continue to overlook the inherent value of platforms like Twitter, Facebook, Instagram and countless others.

As a longtime social media strategist, I have worked with some of the most recognizable brands in a variety of different industries. During this time, I have used my expertise to demonstrate how to properly leverage a social media presence in order to reach a broad range of consumers while simultaneously generating significant revenue through various monetization strategies. Over the years, more and more platforms have been created and now offer a variety of opportunities for monetization while providing access to some very specific key demographics that are essential to the success of any business in any industry.

The monetization strategies I will outline in this book are based on my experience as a corporate social media strategist, but that does not mean these strategies overlook individual users who are looking to monetize what may already be a strong social media presence. The strategies I have developed are designed to benefit individuals and businesses alike, and I will discuss how many of these strategies can be used to achieve any number of financial goals.

Too Valuable to Overlook

When I first began working as a social media strategist, I was surprised to learn just how little emphasis was being placed on leveraging social media for financial gain. I thought companies would immediately recognize the minimal cost of using social media along with the potential for a sizable return on investment on what I believe is the ideal platform for reaching consumers, but it took quite a bit of convincing on my part before companies became willing to expand their efforts. Given the potential benefits of a strong social media presence, the opportunities for monetization are simply too valuable to overlook.

The same can be said of individuals who have eschewed developing a social media presence for whatever reason. Entrepreneurs who do not work on developing a strong following on social media are missing out on one of the greatest opportunities to build brand recognition and to create additional streams of revenue, especially when one considers that social media platforms are often the primary destination for Internet users and serve as the gateway to the rest of the online world. Since many platforms tend to cater to a specific demographic, targeted social media use can allow entrepreneurs to reach the audience most likely to be interested in their product or service.

Opportunities Abound

Social media users that have already developed a strong following but have not implemented any monetization strategies are missing out on an incredibly lucrative opportunity to generate revenue through a platform they likely began using for personal entertainment. Since these users clearly have a knack for communicating with an audience and developing a loyal following, making the move toward monetization only makes sense. Despite this sound reasoning, these platforms remain largely untapped and represent a sort of Wild West for those ready to take advantage of this incredibly lucrative opportunity.

Even the most shrewd corporations are still figuring out the best way to monetize their social media presence, with most continuing to favor the indirect model in which they market their product or services to the consumers that follow them. While there is certainly nothing wrong with taking advantage of the marketing capabilities provided by social media, these corporations could benefit even more by employing some of the more direct monetization strategies I will detail in the chapters that follow.

One of the most important aspects of social media use is staying ahead of the curve with regard to burgeoning platforms while continuing to properly leverage the established platforms that remain popular among users. While there are many platforms deserving of attention, this book will focus on each of the following social media platforms, as they are the ones that represent the best opportunities both now and in the near future:

- Twitter
- Facebook
- Snapchat
- LinkedIn
- Tumblr
- Pinterest
- Instagram
- Vine
- Google+

Each chapter will discuss the demographic makeup of the social media platform's users while providing specific strategies for building a presence that can be monetized to great success. There will also be detailed instructions regarding how users with an established following can implement monetization strategies without alienating their followers or radically changing the way they use their social media account.

Easily Applied Strategies Focusing on Achieving Sensible Goals

The goal of this book is simple and straightforward: To show you the best way to make money while using social media. The strategies I will outline as they relate to each platform are designed to be of benefit to new social media users along with longtime social media users, with a focus on creating a sustainable stream of revenue and maintaining a strong following. Long-term growth is far more important when it comes to monetization, so these strategies will favor this outcome rather than focusing on generating an immediate financial gain that harms the long-term goals of the user.

These strategies are indeed based on a goal-oriented approach, but the goals are not just financial in nature. In order to ensure long-term success, social media has to be used in a way that not only generates revenue, but also attracts followers and creates a sense of trust between all of the involved parties. In this book, I have done my very best to clearly outline the kind of methods that engender trust while still yielding a strong financial outcome.

Twitter

Twitter is one of the most popular social media platforms around and boasts such a broad user base because it remains an entirely free service and is quite simple to use. Though messages are capped at 140 characters per tweet, the limited nature of this platform appeals to users who are looking for a quick way to scroll through their feed to find the most relevant or most interesting information. With close to a billion registered Twitter accounts, the vast audience accessible to users of this platform makes it possible to apply a variety of simple strategies for monetization with great success.

Of course, just signing up for Twitter and sending out tweets does not guarantee any kind of exposure at all, and it is necessary for Twitter users to build up enough followers to make their account valuable enough to generate revenue. In this chapter I will go over some easy methods for quickly building a dedicated following along with how to properly leverage the value of that following through shrewd monetization strategies. Given the ease and accessibility of Twitter, this platform is one of the best options for anyone seeking to create a revenue stream through social media.

A Popular Platform

With the forced brevity of tweets and the constantly updated feed, Twitter is often the first landing spot for Internet users. This means that their online behavior is almost entirely dictated by what shows up in their Twitter feed, thereby creating a valuable opportunity for anyone who is able to offer access to a significant number of accounts. For users with a large following already in place, this means that monetization is possible on an immediate basis. Those without an established following will have to put in some effort to develop a devoted following by understanding the nuances of the platform. Regardless of the source, Twitter users tend to most appreciate the accounts that are capable of simultaneously entertaining and informing, so users of this platform should make that a specific goal of the content they provide.

Necessary Steps Before Monetization

Before you are able to even consider monetizing your Twitter account, it is absolutely critical to have a following in excess of four figures. Fortunately, building a following of this size and greater is not all that difficult with a dedicated approach and the ability to offer entertaining and interesting information. Your first focus should be on demonstrating why you would be a "good follow," which means you are able to share interesting information that a follower may not have found elsewhere, or to share a unique perspective on a topic relevant to their interests.

With solid content in place, you can attract a large audience by following other Twitter accounts that you believe would be interested in your particular message. While not every account will reciprocate by following your account, there is a large percentage that will do so automatically along with countless others that will at least inspect what their newest follower has to say before making a decision. With a bit of promotional work you should be able to attract a following large enough to be able to monetize your account to a significant degree, but you also have to keep in mind just how important it is to maintain your following while doing so. It is therefore essential to understand the value of adopting a nuanced approach to monetization.

Simple Monetization Strategies

The strategies for monetizing your Twitter account are quite simple, but that does not mean it is without the risk of making critical mistakes. An over-leveraged account can quickly cause many of your followers to dismiss it as spam or a bot designed only to sell a particular product or service. In order to successfully monetize your account over a long period of time, you have to use your account primarily to inform and entertain your followers while only occasionally applying a strategy for monetization. The moment your followers begin to feel that the space you occupy in their Twitter feed is not useful they will cease to grant you that space any longer. You will then find that you have to suffer the indignity of being "unfollowed."

Before detailing how to adopt a nuanced approach to monetization, it is important to explain each of the options available to you. The most obvious is selling space on your platform, but you have to be quite careful in doing so. Too many sponsored tweets will cause you to lose followers and will limit your future opportunities, so be cautious about the sponsors you accept and the frequency with which you use your account for promoting third-party products or services. There are a few simple services that make securing sponsorships fairly simple, including each of the following:

- SponsoredTweets.com
- MyLikes Social Publisher
- TweetPeddler
- PaidPerTweeter

In addition to these services you may also want to consider opting for an affiliate marketing program. Once you have established a level of trust with your followers, you can begin recommending relevant products or services by posting a link along with your tweets. When your followers take your advice and buy a product or service through the link you shared, you will receive a nice commission in exchange for your efforts.

Since you are able to choose the programs you work with and can select only products or services you believe in or feel are relevant to your followers, you can make sure you do not compromise your account while generating a nice level of income. With a large following that trusts what you have to say, it is possible to generate a solid stream of revenue through this particular strategy.

The other monetization strategy to consider is not necessarily one that directly generates results, but it is still worth mentioning. Many Twitter users will barter with others that have a following they would like to reach. You may wish to seek out an account with a relatively small audience that happens to be made up of a target demographic if they would be willing to recommend a product or service of yours in exchange for recommending that your followers consider following their account. This quid pro quo strategy therefore allows you to reach an audience that is not necessarily represented by your followers while providing something of benefit to another account and its followers.

Facebook

As the social media platform that led the way as the first to reach such a wide range of users, Facebook has maintained its status as one of the most popular social networking sites and is rife with opportunities for monetization. Facebook will allow you to develop a deep understanding of your target market's unique interests while also providing the opportunity to connect with an incredibly vast and diverse audience. The monetization strategies available through the use of Facebook are vast and are easily applied due to the platform's status as one of the most frequented sites on the Internet.

An Established and Recognizable Brand

The fact that Facebook has been around for so long and has penetrated the market so thoroughly is a tremendous advantage. When you employ monetization strategies through Facebook there is the obvious benefit of reaching a base of users entirely comfortable with the platform and more likely to trust your brand due to its association with a platform they have come to thoroughly understand and trust.

The comfort of users makes marketing and monetization strategies more likely to work when used in conjunction with Facebook, but there is also the issue of saturation and changing demographics. The average Facebook user is beginning to trend more toward an older demographic, with younger users tending to favor other social media sites that are more in tune with the changing platform needs of the demographic.

While this means that the younger demographic is less likely to use the site as a primary social media platform, Facebook remains relevant enough that the members of this valuable group still use the site and maintain active profiles. Facebook therefore represents one of the best platforms for reaching a wide range of people occupying various demographics, making it an excellent tool for monetization.

Beyond Making Connections

One of the most obvious benefits of using Facebook is the ability to make connections with people who are interested in your brand. Personal connections are exceptionally valuable, but Facebook also generates increased trust among users and establishes a level of brand recognition that is not always so easy through other social media platforms. While these developments are important for anyone looking to monetize a social media platform, they remain an indirect means of generating revenue that have to be leveraged in other ways to be truly valuable.

Options for Monetizing Facebook

There are several different options available to successfully monetize a Facebook page, but the most obvious and perhaps most successful is through the use of direct sales. Obviously, this requires that you are selling a product or service, so this is primarily a strategy to be used by business owners and entrepreneurs looking to peddle their wares to an established marketplace. Since many businesses already have a website set up that offers their products or services, creating a whole new Facebook page from scratch would be both time-consuming and redundant, but simply linking to the existing page would also represent an inefficient strategy. Fortunately iFrame exists for this precise reason, allowing users to create a Facebook tab that brings the existing page into the Facebook platform quickly and easily. From there, users can operate in the same way they would on the original site while still remaining on the social media platform they know and trust.

Using direct sales in this way alone is not enough to generate significant results, so using the "Pin to Top" promotional strategy and implementing a widget that makes payment simple is also beneficial for monetizing a

Facebook page. Paypal and Amazon both have widgets that can be used through a Facebook page, and the brand recognition of these options offers the added benefit of further enhancements in consumer trust.

In terms of marketing direct sales through the Facebook platform, it is absolutely necessary for you to target mobile users by making sure your page is designed for use on mobile devices. Whenever you see a person mindlessly gazing into a Smartphone, it is almost always the case that they are scrolling through one of the various social media platforms. Failing to ensure your page is adaptable to a mobile device severely limits your access to Facebook users, so make this a priority right from the start.

With a mob le-friendly page and an easy-to-use direct sales platform, using the right promotional strategies becomes all the more critical. Facebook allows you to post and promote time-sensitive sales and to utilize the deals widget, so make sure you take advantage of these valuable sales tools if you have a product or service to sell on Facebook. It is also highly beneficial to create an opt-in page for a mailinc list through Facebook, and there are several applications that make doing so quite simple. The following apps are designed for this express purpose:

- Aweber
- Constant Contact
- GetResporse
- iContact
- MailChimp

Video Content Creation

One of the most recent developments for Facebook has been the development of a new video platform intended to rival YouTube's long-established dominance. Given the fact that YouTube has been offering bonuses to its content creators to sign an exclusive contract, Facebook appears to be a serious and credible threat. It has long been the case

11

that YouTube has represented one of the most lucrative options for video creators with a large following in place, so it only stands to reason that the same will be true of Facebook's platform.

If you are able to attract a large audience to your Facebook page already, then moving your content to the video medium would be wise. As a relatively new development and with YouTube looking to lock down its established content creators, there should be an opportunity to take advantage of gaining an early foothold in this burgeoning market, especially if you are able to create content that serves your own promotional goals while successfully entertaining your audience to the degree necessary to generate sizable revenue.

Snapchat

As a social media platform, Snapchat has succeeded by operating in a slightly different manner than its competitors by using messages set to expire after a relatively brief period of time. Though the impermanence of this messaging style seems counterintuitive for monetization purposes, there are actually quite a few reasons why Snapchat is a valuable tool for those looking to generate revenue through the use of social media.

The misconception regarding Snapchat s potential value is one of the primary reasons why it is important to properly leverage this platform, as it possesses monetization potential that remains largely untapped. While Facebook and Twitter are popular options for those looking to apply strategies for monetization, the fact that those platforms are already so heavily saturated makes it quite difficult to be heard. Even with plenty of likes, friends and followers, many users find that these audiences can be quite passive and quickly pass over what they have to say without much thought or effort. This is not the case with Snapchat.

As with any other platform, the key to success is to build a strong following. The difference between Snapchat and other platforms, however, is that users are not able to attract or maintain an audience while posting sub-standard content. Fans of your brand on Snapchat expect exceptional content and will quickly abandon you if you are not able to provide content that is worthy of their immediate attention. More so than other platforms, consistently outstanding content is imperative in order to generate revenue on Snapchat.

The Value of a Captive Audience

The most obvious value with regard to Snapchat's platform is the immediacy of the communication style and the fact that you are able to reach only those who are genuinely interested in you or your brand. Since snaps are impermanent, they demand the immediate and complete attention of the user, meaning that you can be far more efficient in communicating an important message. While Twitter followers can easily scroll past your tweets without much thought, Snapchat users understand that they will only get one chance to view your message before it is permanently deleted.

In keeping with this theme of immediacy, Snapchat also enables its users to provide instantaneous, real-time feedback, providing you with valuable and actionable data regarding the efficacy of your message. With devoted fans making up what is essentially a captive audience, your social media strategies are far more likely to be effective through the use of Snapchat. This makes promoting a product or service that much easier, and direct sales are far more likely to generate exceptional results when using the Snapchat platform.

Easy-to-Use Platform

Using this social media platform is simple and allows for the use of varied mediums that include audio, video, photography and artistic renderings. The drawing tools and the camera tools included in the user interface are intuitive for even the least technologically inclined user, making it very easy to employ new and unique methods for communicating with your audience. The user interface makes it possible to create an overarching narrative with a series of snaps, generating even greater interest in the message you are ultimately sending and increasing the likelihood of being able to successfully monetize your brand through Snapchat.

Even though the platform is unique and simple to use, it is not without its drawbacks. The most obvious is the fact that Snapchat is behind when it comes to in-application buy buttons, which many other social media platforms have already integrated. There are some indications that buy buttons are not all that far off, but for the time being you can still link from the snap to an off-app purchasing platform. It is not the most efficient method for monetization, but it is still an effective strategy for this particular platform.

Marketing to the Most Devoted Fans of Your Brand

As previously noted, the primary benefit of Snapchat is the fact that you only attract those who are most devoted to your particular brand and are therefore most deeply interested in your message. This means that you are always marketing to the people who are most receptive and actively interested in buying whatever it is you are selling. A smaller audience on Snapchat is often capable of generating greater conversions than a larger audience on Facebook or Twitter, with the difference essentially being the quality of your Snapchat audience versus the quantity of your Twitter or Facebook audience.

Marketing in this way is more efficient not just because of the inherent loyalty of the audience you have built on Snapchat, but also because the expiring message creates a sense of urgency that changes the way the message is viewed. Due to this perceived urgency, you are far more likely to generate results with a convincing call to action -- users are less likely to ignore the message or put it off until later simply because of the impermanent nature of the platform's messaging system.

Potential for Growth Through SnapCash

The drawbacks of the Snapchat platform have already been mentioned, with the primary limitation currently being the lack of a buy button urging users to take immediate action on the sale of a product or service. While SnapCash currently exists as a user-to-user means of sending money, it is very likely that this service could expand in the near future for commercial purposes as well. Having an audience in place along with an established brand that users know and trust will place you well ahead of the curve when

SnapCash expands in this way, and other brands will be racing just to build a captive audience of their own while yours is already in place and loyal to you. This is a tremendous advantage in terms of monetizing your brand through this social media platform, representing yet another reason why Snapchat is a more valuable platform than most people believe it to be.

LinkedIn

LinkedIn is often overlooked by those looking to monetize social media platforms, but this professional networking site is ideally suited for a variety of effective strategies for generating solid social media revenue streams. The main benefit of this particular platform is the ability of users to identify and target the specific parties that may be interested in their brand, and the search function available through the site is particularly effective for narrowing down a focus to make any monetization strategy that much more efficient.

With well over 200 million users, LinkedIn is not nearly as sizable as some of the other available platforms, but despite this relative lack of size LinkedIn's users tend to be much wealthier on average than the average Facebook or Twitter user. The ability to target an audience that is likely to have an income over six figures means that monetization strategies have the potential to be every bit as effective as any other social media platform, making LinkedIn an important site for building and leveraging your brand.

Promoting Your Brand Through LinkedIn

There are several ways to build your professional network through LinkedIn with the ultimate goal of monetizing your brand, and it is certainly advisable to take a diverse approach in order to achieve the best possible outcome. As a professional network, LinkedIn attracts users looking to exchange ideas and information, so it is important to create content that is clearly valuable in order to build a strong and consistently active network. The platform allows users to create and promote articles on the site that include links to affiliate programs, external websites and, of course, your professional profile.

Promoting your brand by offering the community something of value is a great way to start. In addition to the ability to create blog posts, LinkedIn also allows users to join or

17

create groups based on some unifying aspect of its members. These groups are critical for building a network, and they can also be used to promote and sell products or services -- as long as they are highly relevant and useful to the group.

One of the more important sections of a LinkedIn profile is the projects and publications section. This section of your profile allows you to update your network regarding any new work and is particularly effective when used to promote giveaways or free publications. Informational products are a great way to introduce your expertise while also demonstrating your willingness to give something valuable to the community. When using LinkedIn for monetization purposes, it is important to show how you are able to benefit the community you are attempting to profit from.

The search function provided by LinkedIn also makes it quite simple to target sponsors or advertisers for a blog or website outside of the social media platform. Simply narrow down the search results so that they align with the kind of users that would benefit from sponsoring or advertising on your site. With a targeted search, recruiting paying advertisers and sponsors is quick and easy, especially since the prospective advertisers can quickly recognize the benefit you are offering by inspecting your previous publications and viewing your professional profile.

Affiliate Marketing Opportunities

Using affiliate marketing through LinkedIn is remarkably similar to the other platforms that also offer this opportunity, but LinkedIn does provide some unique qualities that can yield even greater results with the right approach. The key is to understand how to adopt a nuanced approach to affiliate marketing through LinkedIn, as there is a risk of doing too much and alienating your professional network in the process.

The articles and blog posts you write should include affiliate marketing links with relative frequency, but only when it is possible to do so organically and in a way that is highly relevant to the topic you are discussing. Cramming posts full of affiliate links that have only a tenuous connection to the topic will surely drive your audience away, so use discretion by promoting these links only when they truly serve an obvious benefit.

Perhaps the best way to use affiliate marketing on LinkedIn is through the groups you form or are a part of. Instead of beginning a post with an affiliate link, try to only respond to the questions of others by posting a link to an article you wrote featuring an affiliate link. Of course, your responses should be helpful and relevant to the original question, and you should be clear about why the product or service you link would be of benefit. You should offer your help to other users whenever possible, but you should only mention an affiliate product or service when it is clearly appropriate, as this is the best way to ensure you are able to maintain your reputation within your professional network.

Leveraging Network Contacts

LinkedIn is designed for professional networking, and there are monetization opportunities available through several simple networking strategies. The mailing list represents one of the most valuable tools available to those who have informational products to sell, and LinkedIn provides an excellent way to add subscribers to a mailing list. Obviously, you should not simply add those in your professional network without permission, but you do have the opportunity to demonstrate why it would be beneficial for those in your network to subscribe to your mailing list. If you have consistently posted valuable information to your publications page and have been a meaningful contributor to your groups, then recruiting mailing list subscribers should be quite easy.

Once you have a healthy mailing list in place, there are a

lot of ways to leverage the list for additional monetization purposes. Advertisers and sponsors love mailing lists and are more than willing to pay up for valuable space in your newsletter, and any products or services you wish to market to your subscribers can be done quickly and easily through one of the most efficient methods available.

Tumblr

Tumblr is a blogging platform that tends to attract bloggers with an audience most interested in brief and informal content. A popular platform that has been acquired by Yahoo!, Tumblr is a site in which memes and other kinds of image-oriented content thrive, as the user demographics trend toward the young, Internet-savvy generation. This means that a monetization strategy for Tumblr has to take into account the majority of the platform's audience. A serious blogger, for example, is very unlikely to develop the kind of Tumblr following to make monetization efforts worthwhile.

The more than 250 million blogs hosted by Tumblr tend to be relatively short (even by Internet standards) and dense with images, but this is highly advantageous due to the fact that this is precisely the type of content most likely to go viral. Tumblr is therefore one of the best platforms for promoting your brand and building an audience in short order, as sharing through the site is made exceptionally easy among users through the popular 'reblogging" feature.

Attracting a following on Tumblr is quite simple for this reason, as you can follow and reblog established users with the hope that they reciprocate by promoting your work. If you produce good content worth sharing, it is very likely that it will spread quickly and earn you the audience you will need before you can successfully monetize this popular blogging platform. Many of the traditional strategies apply for monetizing Tumblr, but there are a few unique options along with some very important guidelines that have to be taken into account before moving to generate income.

Adopting a Nuanced Approach to Monetization

Tumblr is a little different than some of the other popular hosting platforms. While most do not do very much at all to discourage users from making money, Tumblr is clearly against allowing users to operate with monetization as a *primary* goal. If you try to use Tumblr for the sole purpose of creating a source of revenue, then it will not be too long before you run afoul of the site's rules and regulations. This is especially true for those trying to mislead or deceive readers for the purpose of achieving some financial end, but that does not mean Tumblr is completely anti-monetization.

The site does allow its users to generate revenue through the blogging platform but only if the focus remains on producing quality content that is not always primarily geared to generating revenue. Users have to strike a balance between the kind of content produced solely for the benefit of other users and the kind of content that is created for the purpose of generating revenue. The rules that Tumblr has in place essentially force users to abide by best practices for monetization, as it is always best to avoid over-leveraging a site by focusing on creating a valuable audience experience while only occasionally pushing for monetization. Tumblr's rules are therefore simple to follow, but it nonetheless remains worth noting.

Creating Content for Tumblr

To make the most out of any monetization strategy, you have to build an audience and consistently demonstrate the value of whatever it is you happen to be offering through your brand. While using Tumblr, this means that you are able to create humorous, viral-style content that is worth sharing with other users. The main appeal of the platform is its visual focus and the likelihood of finding silly and fun content that can be quickly shared with others in order to achieve a laugh, so you have to focus on creating this sort of content while also promoting your brand and selling products or services that bring in revenue.

There are many different ways for approaching this, but the simplest and most effective method for ensuring your content is Tumblr-oriented is to limit your level of seriousness and focus on funny content that is visually appealing. This is particularly imperative since many Tumblr users access the platform through their mobile device and are only interested in brief, visually dense content specifically designed for mobile sharing.

Specific Strategies for Monetization

Monetization on Tumblr is relatively simple and straightforward, though you do have to be cautious with regard to the frequency of the strategies you implement in order to keep from appearing to be primarily focused on monetization. Affiliate marketing has to be done in a more nuanced sort of way, but it is still permitted and remains every bit as effective through Tumblr. When choosing an affiliate partner, simply make sure to consider the product or service you will be promoting with regard to the audience you are most likely to reach. Affiliate programs that offer the kind of products and services frequently sought by the young, tech-savvy demographic found on Tumblr will likely be your best option.

Traditional advertising is also available through Tumblr, with popular programs like Google Adsense easily applied to your blog. You can also solicit direct advertising for use on your Tumblr account, but it does require some knowledge of coding to place the advertisement on the site. While advertising in this way remains a strategy worth pursuing, the most valuable form of advertising available through Tumblr is likely self-promotion.

Since Tumblr makes sharing among users simple so content spreads quickly and efficiently throughout the site and beyond, promoting your work among Tumblr users may be the most valuable monetization strategy. If you are a graphic artist or a web designer, for example, each post you create brings significant exposure and can include a link back to a site where you sell your products or services. The same is true of visual artists, and many writers have even promoted their work on Tumblr by taking a brief excerpt or

23

quote from a new book and placing the text over a shareable image. This strategy can generate significant interest in the work you have created and may represent one of the quickest and most efficient promotional strategies, especially when it comes to reaching the demographic typical of Tumblr users.

Pinterest

Once the ideal platform for an affiliate marketing monetization strategy, Pinterest has made a number of changes that have left many of its users scrambling to find new ways to generate revenue through the digital "pinboard" that the site has made so very popular. The website's goal has always been to inspire its users to try new things by creating a community in which ideas are shared and users can quickly and easily learn how to do something new and exciting, and it has stated that the new changes are simply designed to reflect this goal.

The changes are due to the company believing that the marketing behaviors of users increasingly contributed to a suboptimal user experience. While these changes have made it a bit harder to generate revenue through Pinterest, the photo- and video-sharing platform remains a profitable option provided that users are willing to explore new strategies to continue to leverage Pinterest's popularity among visitors.

The visual appeal of the site and the useful information it hosts have made Pinterest a frequent destination of some valuable target demographics, including young, educated women who are financially secure. Pinterest's demographics represent a very specific target market of a host of companies, which is why affiliate programs became so popular among users of the site. Even with the changes recently made to Pinterest's platform, there is a tremendous opportunity to generate a great deal of revenue by targeting the site's key demographic through the strategies that remain unaffected by the changes.

Do Pinterest's Long-Term Goals Align With Monetization Goals?

Many long-term Pinterest users -- particularly those who had already developed a following and were generating significant income through monetization strategies --

reacted poorly to the changes made by Pinterest. The company has made it quite clear that it wants to remain true to its original conception by serving as an aspirational site where users are exposed to new ideas that can be easily applied to their own lives. It has expressed a desire to avoid becoming an ecommerce site like Amazon and believes it would not be able to thrive in such a marketplace even if it did possess that desire. As a result, Pinterest has modified its terms of service to keep the site aligned with its original intentions.

The question then becomes whether or not those intentions align well with monetization strategies. The site has added "buyable pins" on a widespread basis, but that seems to be a strategy that benefits company monetization and not user monetization. Since the company has installed buyable pins while removing all affiliate links from user-generated content, many believe that the site sees user monetization as a threat to the company's own monetization goals. If that is the case, then it seems likely that users will be quite hamstrung with regard to any future monetization strategies as well. Fortunately, that does not appear to be true and there are effective strategies to employ that will be able to generate enough revenue to be more than worthwhile even without affiliate links.

No More Affiliate Links? No Problem!

The major change that has irked many longtime users is the banning of all affiliate links, including those that have already been pinned to the site. The pins remain in place in their original form, but any links to affiliate products or services have been entirely removed. For those who have already put in the hard work to create valuable pins that generate sizable revenue, it is completely understandable that there is quite a bit of consternation. Despite the lack of affiliate marketing opportunities, there are still plenty of options available to pinners who have a large following and are skilled in using Pinterest to create valuable content, including:

- Pinboard curating
- Social media marketing
- Original content creation

Users who have a board in place but are unable to find the time to manage it are more than willing to pay someone to curate the board for them, and it is fairly easy to promote yourself in this way through your own pinboard. The same is true of content creation, as Pinterest remains an important promotional tool for many businesses, especially those that cater to the site's key demographics. Finally, there are always a wealth of paid social media marketing opportunities involving Pinterest that users can take advantage of in order to generate some solid income despite not being able to engage in affiliate marketing programs.

Still an Outstanding Promotional Tool

Just because you cannot promote someone else's products or services in exchange for a nice commission does not mean that you can no longer use Pinterest to promote and sell products and services of your own. This platform remains one of the very best promotional tools around because you are able to show everything that can be done with a particular product or service through the pictures and videos you pin to your board.

If you have a product to sell, consider making a relatively brief video in which you demonstrate how your product can be used in a variety of different ways. You can give away an ebook providing step-by-step instructions for different projects in exchange for subscribing to your mailing list, or you can simply refer viewers to an external site (or, eventually, a buyable pin) where your product can be purchased directly.

If you sell a digital product, you can create a video in which you provide step-by-step instructions for using a widely available material followed by an invitation to learn about other projects using the same material via an eBook you have available for sale. For example, a user could create a video showing how to make Adirondack chairs out of wooden pallets, followed by an invitation to buy an eBook titled "10 Great Projects for Repurposing Wooden Pallets."

Even though Pinterest has made monetization a bit tougher for its users, there are plenty of opportunities to generate income through the use of this creative-themed platform. It is easy to recognize through videos and photos when a pinner is able to offer something of value to their followers, so users that focus on monetization strategies for Pinterest will be able to continue to reap a solid reward.

Instagram

The eminently popular photo-sharing social media platform now features video as well, and, at 15 seconds in length, it appears Instagram continues to be intent on taking the best of every social media platform and trying to do it better than all the others. Instagram has indeed succeeded in combining many of the most popular elements of Twitter, Facebook, Flickr and Vine, resulting in a following of well over 300 million users. With a wide audience and a clear desire to continually improve upon its platform, Instagram represents an excellent opportunity for anyone looking to monetize their social media account.

If you already have an Instagram account, then you are very likely following someone who is making the bulk of their income using Instagram, whether it is as a marketer or as a method for promoting their work. The value of your Instagram account -- as with any other social media platform -- is directly tied to the strength of your following but it is not just sheer numbers that are needed to properly monetize this photo-sharing platform. Understanding the role played by the demographic makeup of your audience is also important for an optimal monetization strategy, as the "who" is just as important as the "how many" when it comes to determining the potential value of your account.

What Is the Value of Your Influence?

Even big-time social media influencers should recognize the value of understanding the demographic makeup of their audience, as this is the best way to ensure their Instagram account is properly leveraged. Accounts in excess of one million followers likely include a healthy cross-section of the consumer population, but that does not mean any account of that size is going to have the cache necessary to convince an engineer that it is time to invest in a new set of calipers. It is therefore important to understand who your followers are, what they are likely to be interested in and whether they would act on the advice you give regarding a particular product or service.

If you are able to recognize precisely where your influence lies, you will be able to leverage the value of your account to a significant degree. While the precise value is likely to differ depending on a number of factors (including the specific demographics of your audience), it has been estimated that accounts boasting more than 500,000 followers can bring in up to $3,000 per photo. Even accounts that have only recently reached the six-figure mark in followers can generate close to $1,000 per photo, provided, of course, that the account finds the right sponsor and is able to demonstrate the value of their influence over a particular audience.

Without followers, it is much harder to properly monetize an Instagram account. Niche followings can still do very well without massive numbers, but it is always best to work to build a strong following. Creating an interactive campaign, for example, can be exceptionally effective as a strategy for building a base of followers. With a strong campaign convincing users to share photos of themselves along with a memorable hashtag, your following can grow at an exponential rate. Once that following is in place, you can then begin to leverage the value of the loyal audience you have successfully attracted.

How to Optimize Instagram Links

Instagram only recently made links clickable, which is an excellent development for anyone looking to monetize their account. Even though cutting and pasting a link from Instagram into a web browser is not exactly a great deal of work, many users will ignore a link unless they are able to click it right then and there. While the addition of clickable links has helped, it is still necessary to optimize any link by keeping it brief and easily recognizable for users. It is also beneficial to make sure any link directs the user to a mobile-friendly page since so many Instagram users access the platform via a mobile device.

Promotions and Sales Opportunities

Photos and videos will always remain some of the most effective promotional strategies for any brand, and the Instagram platform is perfectly suited for use as a digital advertisement that also includes a link to the product or service being promoted. If you have such a product or service, there are plenty of ways to use photos and videos to generate conversions from those in your audience, but you should also try to generate exposure beyond your existing network. Using a shareable hashtag is a great way to accomplish this.

As an example, you can offer a free product or service you happen to be introducing for sale to the user who posts the best photographic evidence of why they are most deserving of the product or service while including your hashtag in the post. By encouraging your followers to be creative in sharing silly pictures, you are more likely to get significant exposure for the product or service you are trying to promote for sale.

There are other ways to promote just about anything, particularly since Instagram can be used as a digital portfolio. This extends beyond just photographers and graphic artists, as any professional can benefit from a visual representation of their work or experience. With the addition of video, users can now create brief commercials or previews of webinars that followers may be interested in. There are even some apps that can be used in conjunction with Instagram to create an additional sales channel just by using a simple hashtag with the post.

Affiliate Marketing, of Course

There are several ways to use affiliate marketing through Instagram, but it is still necessary to avoid misleading or misrepresenting any affiliate activity by simply noting it as such. Clickable links to affiliate products or services can be included in Instagram posts, or you can link to a blog post you wrote that already includes affiliate links.

Instagram users have found it quite effective to promote an affiliate product or service by sharing pictures and videos serving as proof of its value. You can also encourage your followers to post their own pictures with the affiliate product and create a collage demonstrating its varied uses and the benefit it has brought for so many others. How successful these efforts are, of course, continues to depend on your ability to balance the use of your Instagram account so you are generating income while still providing valuable content for your followers to enjoy.

Vine

Vine is a relatively new entrant to the social media landscape, with its looping videos lasting just six seconds but still offering users the opportunity to create entertaining content precisely because of the limitations the platform has imposed. The brief videos are popular because they are so shareable -- users understand that viewing an individual Vine will never feel like a waste of time even if it falls well short of expectations. Viners that are able to create consistently entertaining content can build a following in short order, and, of course, a devoted following is always necessary when it comes to monetizing a social media account.

There are some limitations, however, as the range of monetization strategies to be employed through Vine are not as vast as some other platforms. Despite these inherent limitations, there is a lot of money to be made through Vine provided you are able to break through and build the kind of audience that wields a lot of power over companies looking to reach those who happen to make up your audience. Understanding why Vine is such a popular platform is essential to building up an audience or adding followers to an existing audience, as tailoring content creation to attract followers is a key step to ultimately monetizing your social media account.

The Power of (Repeating) Brevity

The limit of six seconds still provides more than enough time for the viewer to capture everything they need from a particular video and allows the creator ample time to set up a scene in order to convey an emotion or to deliver a hearty punch line. The looping aspect allows viewers to capture what they may have overlooked during the initial viewing while creators can make Vines in which it is difficult to distinguish the beginning from the end. These characteristics are appealing for both viewers and creators, as the content does not have to take very long to produce and it certainly does not take very long to view.

Vine has become a powerful vehicle for branding for this reason. Companies are reaching out to Viners for sponsorships and brand placements, while Viners with large audiences are able to wield a great deal of influence over their followers. The fact that Vine is something of a meritocracy is also quite appealing: The most popular Viners are popular because of Vine and Vine alone. If you are able to create the kind of content that is received well by Viners, then this social media platform is one that can be incredibly lucrative.

Building a Committed Following

Vine's platform can be used to convey just about any message, but the most popular type of content is undeniably comedic in nature. Many of the most popular Vine users opt for an almost slapstick approach, and solid production values are definitely not a requirement for building a devoted following. The goal is to entertain, and Vine seems to attract an audience that prefers a silly type of humor. If you want to build a following on Vine, the best strategy is to focus on creating the kind of entertainment-oriented content that has come to be expected by users of this platform.

Of course, the content has to get noticed in order to attract a following. In order to accomplish this you have to focus on landing your Vine on the popular page or to get others to revine your work. If you succeed in doing this several times over, you will build a strong following in no time at all, giving you the kind of audience that can yield a sizable income just by making a few Vines each week.

Lucrative Sponsorship Opportunities

The main source of income among Viners comes through sponsorships and product placement. Users with a sizable following can earn several thousand dollars for a single Vine despite the inherent brevity of the medium, as companies are recognizing that the typical Vine audience represents an exceptionally important demographic. Viners are the conduit through which these companies can reach this segment of the population, and it further benefits them to have their brand associated with Viners who have built up a great deal of trust in the audience that follows them.

In order to attract sponsors, Viners often turn to agencies to connect them with the brands that are looking for a way to reach a specific segment of the consumer population. Perhaps the most beneficial aspect of the relationship between sponsors and Viners is the fact that there seems to be an understanding that the sponsored content cannot appear anything but organic. Viners are therefore able to maintain the approach that earned them their following in the first place, which makes the relationship between the Viner and the sponsor mutually beneficial. This means you will not have to be concerned about compromising your style or your voice when working with a sponsor.

If you are more interested in using Vine as a promotional tool for your own products and services, then there are options for this approach as well. Many companies use their Vine accounts to offer unique insight into how products or services are created or to provide access to some other behind-the-scenes aspect of the operation. You can promote your products by showing them in action via short video clips, or you can use multiple platforms at once by using a Vine on Twitter (Twitter just so happens to own Vine). Of course, you can also just strive to entertain your audience in however way you choose while promoting your brand in some fashion. With a unique medium and a rapidly expanding base of users, Vine represents a lucrative opportunity for those who are able to properly leverage the value inherent in this social media platform.

Google+

Google's entrant in the world of social media has not been anything close to an unmitigated disaster, but it has certainly not lived up to the lofty expectations associated with everything the tech giant produces. While there is some thought that Google+ can simply be ignored when it comes to monetization efforts, this would be a mistake that causes you to miss out on some financially beneficial opportunities. This is especially the case if you are seeking the audience that Google+ has managed to attract thus far, but there are reasons beyond just reaching a specific demographic that makes it worthwhile to explore the implementation of monetization strategies through this platform.

An Underutilized Platform

It is important to be absolutely upfront about this fact: Google+ does not boast a massive audience and certainly cannot count a younger demographic among its users. For marketers who are always touting the importance of the 18-to-35 demographic, Google+ is not exactly the trendiest of social media platforms. With that being said, there is still tremendous value in using Google+ for monetization, and the platform has a wealth of users worth seeking out and engaging in order to build your brand with the goal of monetizing your social media presence.

Perhaps it is important to look back on the users that achieved the most widespread success on Vine: The most popular Viners not only understand how to use the platform to create content that resonates with other users, but they were also among those who developed a presence on the platform before it exploded in popularity. Since they were already established as Viners worth following, many new users followed them almost by default after setting up a profile of their own. While Google+ is not exactly a new platform, there is still an opportunity to establish a presence before the platform's popularity grows.

Certainly there is no guarantee that Google+ will dethrone the other popular platforms, but it seems like only a matter of time before Google adds the kind of unique feature that will attract new users at an exponential rate. For this reason alone it is a great time to establish a presence worth monetizing on Google+, and the platform is an excellent means for engaging the audience you are trying to reach, especially when using Google Hangouts.

Taking Advantage of Google Hangouts

The Google Hangouts feature of Google+ may be one of the most attractive methods for generating income through informational products and services. This feature makes it incredibly easy to engage your audience on a deeply personal level while also providing a valuable service. Many users who offer informational products through Google+ use Google Hangouts to either deliver their product "in-person" or to create additional value for an existing digital product they offer for sale. A DIYer, for example, might offer an eBook with step-by-step instructions for any number of projects and could add in-person assistance via Google Hangouts for an extra fee.

This extends to anyone selling just about any kind of product or service through Google+, and it is a great way to add value to your existing products or services while creating a personal bond with those who are interested in what you have to offer. Even though Google Hangouts is an excellent platform for webinars and other person-to-person products and services, payment collection is not yet as seamless as it could be. Many users still collect payment through PayPal and make arrangements with clients through Google+, but that is only a minor inconvenience considering the value of the platform itself.

A Promotional Tool

As a promotional tool, Google+ does not yet have the cache

of a Twitter or a Facebook. You won't hear companies asking customers to join a community on Google+ the way you constantly hear requests for Twitter, Facebook and even Instagram, but the platform remains an excellent promotional tool for those whose target market uses Google+. If you are marketing a product or service that appeals to the most popular demographics of Google+, then it is incredibly valuable to promote your brand on this platform through your profile, your posts and your comments. It is in this way that you can drive conversions and push traffic to an external site you use for generating income.

Even if your audience is not on Google+ there is good reason to use the platform as a promotional tool. While there is a lot of division on the subject, it appears Google uses Google+ to help in determining page rankings in search results. Pages that received the most "+1's" on Google+ almost always have a better ranking on search results in Google, and many believe the only thing having an impact greater than "+1's" is the site's page authority.

Along with the fact that the Google search engine "crawls" Google+ immediately, using this social media platform can result in greatly enhanced brand recognition. Even if Google+ does not have as great an impact on search results as some believe, the fact remains that Google can always change the way it ranks a site based on factors taken from its social media platform. In fact, Google may already have an incentive to do this, as it could easily improve participation on Google+ just by making this change to its search engine algorithm -- if, of course, it hasn't done so already.

An Unrestricted Affiliate Marketing Platform

Many of the social media platforms we have discussed have included some sort of restriction regarding the use of affiliate marketing programs, but Google+ does not have any restriction other than the standard federal guideline mandating transparency when promoting a product or service through an affiliate program. Through the use of this unrestricted platform, you can promote your affiliate links throughout Google+, including on your posts and right on your profile as well.

This enables you to gain a greater level of exposure for your affiliate links, but not just on the Google+ platform. Through the use of Google+ authorship, any review or article you write -- including those featuring affiliate links -- grants you a greater level of authority with Google search results and contributes to greatly improved results for your affiliate marketing strategies. When used correctly, Google+ can be an exceptionally lucrative social media option.